MEMOIR OF A MUNCHKIN

UDAY KHANDEPARKAR

ISBN
Paperback 979-8-89610-723-1
Hardcase 979-8-89699-315-5

CONTENTS

Foreword   5

1   From Bombay to Old Brompton Road   9

2   Slow Boat to GOA   12

3   *'Aata Majhi Satakli' Is from a*
    Bollywood Hit Called 'Singham'   17

4   Biker Boys and Their Bravado   19

5   The Nine Nights of Navaratri   22

6   'Gatari Amaavasya'   27

7   How to Get Hair-Ready for
    Navaratri Nights at an Expensive Salon for Free   29

8   Abcd of a Good Career   31

9   A Confession to Make   35

10 Amitabh Bachchan   41

11 London and the Elephant Trunk Pickle   44

12 Lunatics on Earth Too   47

13 If You Ignore This Aberration,
    Ganapati Went Green a Long Time Ago   51

14 Viva Portugal   53

15 You Can Use Coconut Hair Oil
    but No Coconuts on a Plane   55

16 Goan *Susegad* Versus Mangalorean Staunchness   57

17 Wrong Perspectives from the 1980s Corrected Now   63

18 Bombay Prohibition Act, 1949
    and Other Delusions of This City   66

19 Abstinence and Hypocrisy   69

20 On Death and Obits   73

21 By Permission of the *Parmatma*   74

22 Narendra Modi's Sarpa Dosha   77

23 Modi's Vision Is So Far and
    Far-Fetched, You Need a Telescope to Look At It   80

24 The Modi Monetisation Plan
    That Was to Raise a 6 Followed by 12 Zeroes   83

25 The Intangible Hindu Divinity   87

26 The Hindutva Brigade Misunderstands Me   90

27 Playing Games with *Bhakt* and the Barbra Effect   93

28 The Real Practicality of Ancient Hindu Ritual   96

29 Journalism Is Now "Snack-Able Content"   99

30 A Geriatric Tree Officer   102

31 A Go-Air Flight That Went Nowhere for Three Hours   104

32 Maiya to Masala to Money   107

FOREWORD

Munchkin is described in the dictionary as someone notably small and endearing. On the first descriptor, I qualify 100 percent; On the second I try hard to be a dear, as much as is possible. Being small is grossly underrated as an advantage in life. I know this from 1966 when I was six-years-old living in Happy House Chawl in Vakola, Santacruz in Mumbai.

I am serious, it was named Happy House and still exists happily. Regardless of what such dwellings are named whether *Pandurang Villa* or *Mushkil Manzil*, they are all very 'happy houses' to live in as a child.

It is a structure with one long train of a verandah, off which branches break out at 12-feet intervals. They lead to one 100 square-foot room, has a semblance of a doorway in the middle and grandly goes on to another 60 square-foot space that doubles as a kitchen and wash space for all purposes.

The entire entity together is called 'kholi', room, you know! Except for nights when you went in to sleep, the long verandah with 10 homes to the left and another 10 to the right are all yours to wander in and out as you desire.

But I am wandering away from munchkin, a small and timid boy at Happy House's Diwali celebrations when party games were properly gender specific. Knitting competition for girls and robust games for boys - one of which called 'bursting the balloon' that I was pushed into.

They tied balloons behind each small back and then apparently gave instructions that each of us go and bust the other boys' backs. I did not understand a word of what they said and stood quietly in one corner, wondering with index finger on my cute cheek what the pandemonium was all about.

In due course, all other boys' backs were busted and there was one clear victor, Dennis, who had totally overlooked me in my little corner. The Happy House elders goaded him to go after me and that is when I realised that he was after the balloon on my back.

We went round and round together, like a dog chasing its own tail. Very soon the bigger and stronger boy burst my balloon, and everyone applauded.

A little later at the prize distribution, Dennis won an elegant plastic soap box, and I got a tin-crafted red helicopter. Later putting his hand over my shoulder, my dear boyhood friend said: "Chhyya, I should have lost to you."

This memoir is a view of life from that munchkin's corner where you do not necessarily have to exert too much to win a prize.

Just position yourselves properly, like in a crush-hour crowded Mumbai local train. As long as you are somewhere in the centre of that force that wants to get out at Santacruz railway station, you have to do nothing.

Before the train comes to a halt, you will be pushed out on platform number one so far that you are almost at the edge of platform number two to get once again pushed into the reverse train to go right back to Churchgate.

A final word of caution that this book is a hotchpotch of so many different threads that you will get totally lost unless you follow it very very closely. The best warning that I can give on this is by borrowing a line from the National Highway Authority of India that puts up on inter-state highways after every milestone a signboard that reads, "*Dhyan Hatti, Durghatana Ghati*".

Words decoded:

Pandurang	: A Hindu God, considered an avatar of Vishnu
Mushkil	: Difficult
Manzil	: Destination
Mushkil Manzil	: Difficult Destination
Dhyan Hatti, Durghatana Ghati	: Focus Wavers, Accident Occurs

The long verandah of Happy House from the sixties, still stands, but it does not look that happy anymore.

Residents have taken over my clutter-free childhood play area with their chairs, buckets, old rugs, bicycles and rusty window air-conditioners jutting out.

1

FROM BOMBAY TO
OLD BROMPTON ROAD

Fast forward to 28 years later when mentor Jeremy Clift sent munchkin to join that year's Reuters Graduate Trainee Programme for journalists.

The flash forward specifically to 1994 is inspired by train travels, just referred to in the foreword or preamble, which I prefer because it rhymes with amble and ramble which is what this serious shot at literature is designed to do.

On rowdy Mumbai trains, munchkin could gauge accurately amid that sweaty mass of humanity where to put one foot inside the train and let the collective force do the rest of pushing me in. That technique was called 'Find the Gap'.

In London, I encountered a very polite 'Mind the Gap', Mind the Gap,' in a monotone recorded in 1960 in the voice of Oswald

Laurence, a theatre actor. It advised commuters not to fall in the crack between the train step and railway tracks below.

Thank God and British Rail for this because if it were not for this, there is no telling how many goofy Londoners may have fallen in that gap between train above and track below. That English care for commuters was a far cry from Mumbai, then Bombay, where the train had to be careful.

When 200 tons of steel came hurtling into the railway station, men with trousers hitched up and ladies with sari ends wrapped tightly around their waist would lunge forward - one second they were on the concourse and next they were attached to the edge of the train door, still thundering in at 30 kilometres an hour.

It's not fair at all that there is no Olympic event of this kind for we would have taken the gold, silver, bronze as well as the fourth slot on the bench meant for three. But let that be.

This is a tough narrative to narrate. I mean if munchkin starts off with a title that says from 'Bombay to Old Brompton Road' with no reference to it until much later, is not fair. Reuters then was a very generous employer of journalists with first-class international air travel and stays in Chelsea, where billionaires and British royals live.

Old Brompton Road in London was very close to Nell Gwynn House, a serviced apartment, where I resided and took the tube from Knightsbridge to Black Friars to walk to Fleet Street to get trained in reporting and writing by George Short, more on that later.

In office, she is a diligent employee working quietly and on the train station she turns superwoman. It is still speeding into the railway station but she gets in first while others, blurry in the background, wait for it to slow down to a safer speed. Her bags go flailing about but her feet and grip on the train are firm. Truly, a champion!

2

SLOW BOAT TO GOA

Just before you dear reader wander off thinking that I am too much in awe of the British way of life, that is not the case at all. They have decent trains and a staid crossing on the English Channel from Dover this side to French Calais on the other side.

We had a boat Bombay to Goa with a lot more character. They were two rusty old iron tubs, one called *Konkan Shakti*, the other called Konkan *Sevak*. Run by the Shipping Corporation of India, these noisy diesel-powered boats sailed in opposite directions. One went Bombay to Goa, the other plied Goa Bombay.

Sometime in the middle of the dark night, off the Ratnagiri coast in the Konkan they passed each other, and captains of both boats gave two or three sharp toots, awakening all from their *feni*-induced sleep.

The journey was as good as the destination, starting by alighting with our tin trunks at the harbour line Dockyard Road railway station and heading to the appropriately named '*Bhaucha Dhakka*'.

'*Dhakka*', shoves and pushes there used to be aplenty at the big barrier where hundreds of people strained to get into the boat to claim their prime places on the upper and lower decks. Tiny me was no match for the burly, beefy Catholic boys who wrestled like it was a rugby match.

The race was to rush and fling your bed sheet at the spot you wished to claim on the iron floor and that breasting of the tape was honoured by all. If it was your bed linen, that place was yours - no one challenged it. The fight lasted only until all settled down.

After that, it used to be one merry family party with shots of feni in plastic glasses and choriz-pao handed over to total strangers sitting next and 'One Way Ticket to the Moon' playing on Sony two-in-one stereos brought from Abu Dhabi.

The 270-nautical-mile journey took the boat bobbing gently along India's western coast a full 24 hours to reach port on the other side, which mathematically translates to a speed far, far slower than the mackerel fish.

This favourite fish called bangda is a top favourite food of Goans who have it in a spicy tangy curry called *ambot tik*, otherwise pan-fried in a red cafreal masala or a green recheado masala. When *bangda* is alive and swimming, it can race at 80 kilometres per hour.

My delicate enquiries with a ship-captain nephew revealed that when you multiply one nautical mile by 1.852, it gets converted to kilometres. So, 270 x 1.852 = 500: Our boat took 24 hours to cover 500 kilometres, which means it drifted at a speed of 21 kilometres per hour.

Now my math is not very strong as you will spot indications toward later in this book, but as you can see if a tiny bangda can beat a big boat, that is saying something. No match No! If we are going at 20 kilometres per hour and bangda is going four times faster at 80 kmph.

But this speed of sailing fits perfectly with the Goan temperament termed 'susegad' and is loosely understood as a relaxed and laid back-attitude to life, which many non-Goans very wrongly assume is the same as being lazy.

Not at all, certainly not - Goans are not lazy at all, except for three hours each afternoon when a post-lunch nap is taken as mandated by law laid down by the Portuguese, the colonisers, who left Goa in 1961. We respect tradition in its entirety and work hard to achieve susegad, originating from the Portuguese word *sossegado*, which means "quiet" or "calm".

Being calm means you can't be bothered to have a Bombay to Goa race with a bangda. What is the point, when you know that finally when you get there you will eat the little fellow dipped in a spicy sauce.

The boat took a full 24 hours to get to Goa and when I got off, that bobbing feeling stayed with me for the rest of the day.

Words decoded:

Konkan : Name of a coastal region in Maharashtra and Goa

Shakti : Strength

Sevak : Servant

Bhau : Brother

Bhaucha : Belonging to brother

Dhakka : Jetty, also means shoving and pushing

Feni : Goan liquor brewed from either cashew apple or from coconut toddy

Choriz : Spicy pork sausage

Pao : Bread

Bangda : Mackerel fish

Goans take as easily to fluids as a fish does to water. At 3,700 square kilometres, it is India's smallest state area-wise. On the western side is the Arabian Sea, giving Goa some of the best beaches in the world.

Within, Goa has 11 major rivers and 42 tributaries, one of them called Khandepar. This water body and the village on its banks were named after this author's ancestors, or was it the other way around, we are not sure.

The rivers serve like highways with the ferry boat taking people, cars, bikes, market produce and sometimes cattle from one bank to the other.

This water colour sketch by Tushar Shetty, an architect by profession and artist by passion, was inspired by the crossing of the ferry at Betim on the banks opposite Panaji.

3

'AATA MAJHI SATAKLI' IS FROM A BOLLYWOOD HIT CALLED 'SINGHAM'

Fast-forward to 2024 as I do not want to lose young readers who may not have heard of the 1980s 'One Way Ticket to the Moon' on a slow boat to Goa.

This was in the rains just elapsed and I was walking back home, side-stepping a muddy rainwater puddle this side and the piddle of a most adorable Lhasa Apso dog the other side. I now live in one of Mumbai's next-to-be, most-upscale suburban enclaves. Stepping into dung one moment and saying Cho Chweet to expensive pets and their chweeter-still owner-girls is all part of my routine amble back home after buying whisky.

That evening was different and I felt the pain I did 44 years ago as a biker-boy. The young lad came out in jeans and T-Shirt with rubber slippers, very prone to slipping in Mumbai's rain-fed slush.

He held the motorbike handle bar muscularly and kicked hard on the start pedal. Next instant, he winced in pain and I knew the kick-start pedal ricocheted back to get him in the fleshy painful part next to his ankle bone.

'Kick Satakli', the visibly-anguished boy said in Marathi after observing that I was empathising with him. This is a new one added by the author to his collection of 'Aata Majhi Satakli' phrases.

Words decoded:

Satakli : Slipped

Aata : Now

Majhi : My / mine

Aata Majhi Satakli : In this usage, satakli is not slipped but 'lost it', so it translates to: 'Now I'm really pissed off and angry', something like 'You got my goat'.

4

BIKER BOYS AND THEIR BRAVADO

That weak and painful instance of my neighbouring biker boy was rare because at all other times their bravery calls for great admiration. They can take on anything - a 10,000 kg BEST bus or an even heavier-fully-loaded automated cement mixer truck.

My small car is child's play for them, they weave designs around my Maruti Suzuki hatchback with the dexterity of a mosquito, buzzing suddenly on the left, nearly biting my car rear and flying far far away just when I fear colliding into them, not intentionally of course.

Out of respect for them, some road etiquette should strictly be followed by all old and boring car owners. If you, fat cat in a car, are in the slow lane and there is just enough space to move left and go ahead, do not take it. Because thumb rule Number One is always leave an-at least two-feet-wide gap on the left for biker boys to go zipping by, sometimes along with your left rear-view mirror.

That is a small price to pay if our young must survive in the absence of proper jobs. They are delivering someone's much awaited *chole bhature*. I am happy to report gender equality in this matter - I see very well-dressed young girls too doing this though it does not look like they work for an instant-delivery company.

Over time, you will learn that blocking that slender left-most gap is a cardinal sin in the judgement of biker boys. If you ever make that mistake, there will be 21-second pain of heavy honking and a nasty look at you as they pass by saying, *"Kya kar rahe ho, Uncle"*.

Thumb Rule Two when parking outside a street stall with no valet parking and you expect to come back within one minute after buying *anda-pav* is that you have to allocate another ten minutes to be able to get out.

Because by the time you have said: 'Ek dozen anda dena bhai', one biker has delicately steered his steed horizontal, six inches away from your front fender, lifted one long leg in an artistic semi-circular motion, adjusted his pants and walked away. Same behind.

So, until you get a Tesla lateral parking car you wait, patiently, and wonder what causes such actions. I understand and empathise - the heat inside the helmet jellies the delicate matter below and the juddering causes their brains to gradually slip down to where it touches the seat of the bike.

How do I know this? Because I too was a biker boy a long time ago.

Words decoded:

Chole	:	Chickpea stew
Bhature	:	Fine wheat-flour bread deep-fried to look like an inflated balloon
Kya har rahe ho, Uncle	:	WTF are you doing, Uncle
Anda	:	Eggs
Anda dena bhai	:	Eggs please, Bro!
Pav	:	Bread. Note – In Bombay it is spelt pav, in Goa it is spelt pao, though both are pronounced similarly, same to same

5

THE NINE NIGHTS OF NAVARATRI

If it's a young boy on a bike, it won't be long before a cute girl comes along in a stylish blouse above and a pant below that is shredded so badly at the knee as if she fell off the bike even before her first date.

It's a good preemptive move because when she does take a tumble, which eventually will happen, her parents won't know that she was holding on tight to a boyfriend, which caused him to lose balance.

But in the season that just went by when it was *Navaratri*, these girls were all dressed in shiny *ghagra* choli, colour coded for each night, as per planetary positions. Navaratri, meaning nine nights, is dedicated to the nine *avatar* of Goddess Durga. Each day of the week is associated with a specific planet and a prescribed colour.

The Navaratri *mandals*, meaning those in charge of the chaos in the name of the Goddess, very helpfully put up huge hoardings outside their garba grounds indicating the colour of the night.

Like right next to munchkin's mansion measuring 390 square feet *Rera-carpet*, there were boards in Marathi saying '*Shanivar - morpankh nila*', meaning on Saturday wear peacock blue or royal blue.

The specific instructions are much needed and instructive because the sequence does not remain the same in all years from night one to night nine. Our festivals are fixed by the Hindu lunar calendar and Navaratri and Diwali dates vary each year from the Gregorian calendar, depending upon the waxing and waning of the moon.

So what was peacock blue on the first night of Navaratri last year may be fluorescent green this year or even a bright and glossy pink. So, the instruction boards are useful and walking past on night one, I checked on my preparedness for Navaratri, 2024 and put it down in my personal diary, which read like this:

"First day yellow - I have a pale-yellow shirt but no matching yellow pant.

Second day green - I have a bottle-green T-shirt but no bright green pant to match.

Third day grey - I have several grey shirts and pants to change every half hour of dandiya.

Fourth day orange - An orange coloured shirt and pant to match is more than I can take.

Fifth day white - I have several shirts white but no white pants, what to do?

Sixth day red - Next Navaratri I will go buy a red shirt and redder-still pant.

Seventh day royal blue - I have a three-piece suit to wear for *dandiya* dancing.

Eighth day pink - I will give this a pass in both shirt and pant matter.

Ninth day purple - a purple pant? Maybe, Aubergine I'll try next year.

I know these colours are not for me and I love that the young and happy wear all these that signify each virtue of Goddess Durga, whose blessings I took by having a *malai peda prasad* of *Mataji* from a pious temple-going neighbour.

Just one question, what is that instrument they play at garba events. I am told it is bulbul tarang, which is a cross between a two-stringed ukulele, and a typewriter.

"It is a cheap fret board with strings and old Godrej heavy duty typewriter keys on which you get a hideously shrill sound that cuts through ear plugs and sears the soul even when you sit in a room with all doors and windows tightly shut with air conditioner and air purifier on.

I will wear all of the prescribed colours next year if you make them stop playing this bulbul tarang. I promise! *Aai Shapath!*"

End of my Navaratri, 2024 diary entry.

Words decoded:

Nava	:	Nine
Ratri	:	Nights
Navaratri	:	Nine nights
Ghagra	:	A flared skirt for women
Choli	:	A low-cut blouse that ends way above the navel
Mandal	:	Organisers of a cultural or religious event
Rera	:	Real Estate Regulatory Authority, a supervisory body to rein in India's greedy real estate business, where builders counted spaces in the stairways outside as well as the footpath leading to your home as part of your apartment and charged you a king's ransom for what they called 'super built-up'. Rera-carpet now specifies that a builder can charge for only as much space as you can roll out a carpet.
Garba	:	A gyrating group of people where dancers go round and round. Some say garba is the same as karma – what goes around comes around.
Dandiya	:	Same as garba, except that this going round and round happens with two sticks tapped well-timed into two other sticks just passing by on the inner circle.

Malai Peda Prasad	:	A condensed milk round sweet offered to Gods and then considered sacred to eat
Shanivar	:	Saturday
Morpankh	:	Peacock feather
Nila	:	Blue
Mataji	:	Mother, in this case Goddess
Aai shapath	:	I swear by my mother

Round and round, they go, doing the garba dance for nine nights, each of them wearing a specific colour

6

'GATARI AMAAVASYA'

Not all Hindu occasions are such fun, some are outrageously funny. Like 'Gatari Amaavasya". 'Gatar' is gutter and amaavasya is no-moon night, which is the last day of the Hindu lunar month of Aashadh before the holy month of Shravan starts, marking a period of abstinence from meat, fish, eggs and liquor.

The origin of this name is now contested by Hindu purists who detest it saying it casts the religion in bad light. They have of late come out with an elaborate explanation that it is not 'Gatari' but 'Gata aahari', gata being past and aahar meaning diet. In effect saying in the month of Shravan don't have the same diet you had in the past, in the month of Aashadh and so on.

Historic reporting by respected newspapers on this colourful occasion suggests this 'past diet' explanation is pure bunkum. Some mid-nineteenth newspapers said labourers and farmers from the Konkan consumed alcohol brewed locally.

Some of them had more than they could stand and after a while laid on the ground flat, the Marathi word for which is 'Aadavi'. That's why those days it was also referred to as 'Aadavi Amaavasya'. There is no documented evidence of this but you can safely deduce that as Bombay got more and more crowded, there was not much flat ground left to lie in a blissful state of repose. But gutters there were aplenty.

All of Mumbai's cheap bars respect this tradition. Liquor sales that single night stagger twice as much as the previous 30 days of Aashadh and if just the bones of Chicken 65 eaten that night were piled up neatly, it would dwarf a medium-sized mountain.

Chicken 65, a starter to have with very stiff alcoholic drinks, has always intrigued me. I think it is chicken wings dipped in a really hot chilly paste and fried in an even hotter cauldron of oil recycled for several Chickens 65. It is suicidal to eat, but my near and dear love it, so I won't say anything more on this. What qualities entitled it to be numbered 65, I have no idea, but I will let that pass.

Words decoded:

Chicken 65 : Google search, relying on news reports by highly esteemed newspapers like the Times of India, says the name comes from the dish being conceived in 1965 in Chennai, then Madras. Others say they first marinated 65 pieces and some others say, in the army mess menu in Madras, this enigma was listed at number 65. How boring!

They should have named it Chicken 69, allowing for far more interesting observations on its name origin.

7

HOW TO GET HAIR-READY FOR NAVARATRI NIGHTS AT AN EXPENSIVE SALON FOR FREE

I got one such, which was the longest-duration haircut of my life, lasting about an hour to get done what my local barber does in six minutes. I didn't volunteer for it, but circumstances led to it.

My partner saw it on Facebook or some such that a top-notch stylist was offering free haircuts for ladies, which was an offer that looked too good to refuse because Bblunt, the offerer, is a very big chain of luxury salons. It was founded by Adhuna, former wife of actor Farhan Akhtar, later bought out by Godrej Consumer Products Ltd and a little later by Honasa Consumer Pvt. Ltd., the parent company of Mamaearth, a successful beauty brand.

I was a passive observer when I took her to the Bblunt salon on Swami Vivekananda Road in Andheri when Nikita came about all bouncy and said: "Hey! Just give me 10 minutes okay!" Then Nikita looked at me and said: "You too need a haircut". I said "Really!"

She did not wait for me to answer. Went inside to fetch Lily and said she will groom you.

Taken aback by the speed of events, I just nodded my head and went along. It was only when I went into the operation theatre that I realised that this was Bblunt Academy, where they teach enthusiastic and hardworking hairdresser wannabes to cut hair at the right angle in relation to the scalp and the slope of the nape, with the right scissor.

And this was their final practical exam where they got many female heads but male heads were far and few to do their practical examinations on, watched over by a stern supervisor. Now I knew why Lily led me eagerly to her hair-dressing chair.

The bar is set very high at these Salon graduation tests - they are meant to do a diverse range of heads - women curly, women straight, women crooked; Men with moustache, men bearded, men boring, men eccentric.

Lily pulled my hair in the rare places it was still growing and stretched it out between her index and middle finger to give it a gentle cut, a snip here, a snip there! Tough luck, she got a bad question paper with not much hair to answer for.

I gave very generous tips to both Lily and Nikita and made a mental note not to make such a B-blunder again. Right across the high street where I live now, there is another high-end salon called B-bold and I steer clear of it, lest they pull me in for their practical papers.

8

ABCD OF A GOOD CAREER

Hair cutting is very profitable if you place it in the right perspective. Like the CEO of a world-famous watches company was asked by a reporter how the watch and timepiece business was doing and he said: "I have no idea. I don't sell watches. I sell the dream of luxury". Expensive salons are like that – it is not about the haircut; it is about making you feel rich far beyond your means.

Bblunt's last ownership sale was done at some 80 crore rupees, which is about $10 million, not bad at all. But to be able to do that, you need to have Papa's money to set up all those fancy outlets. If you are like middle class munchkin, you just choose more conservative routes.

And here is where I have good advice to give to all our super-brainy 16-year-old girls and boys. To begin, get your ABCD right - without that you won't know where to start in our acronym-crazy country. It all starts at the top, like Modi is not Modi, but Modijee.

Jee is also Joint Entrance Exam that gets you into IIT, Indian Institute of Technology, where you study engineering and then you appear for CAT, WAT and PI to get into IIM because you know how a typewriter works but now you need to learn how to trade derivates at Morgan Stanley.

Let me pause for breath for I have lost track: CAT is common admission test, WAT is written ability test and PI is personal interview which are all necessary to get into IIM, Indian Institute of Management.

If you are an equally brainy teenager of the frog-dissecting type, you must go for NEET, National Eligibility cum Entrance Test to study medicine but be forewarned that JEE, politician-jee is also a tough exam to clear.

Now pay close attention, girls and boys. I am going to instruct you in an alphabet soup that in new age India is far more lucrative as a career than anything your dads and mums have seen before.

It's fun too, like being RJ, radio jockey. This one is called RP, resolution professional, for which you need a simple BCom degree and one of the following, I think - CA, ICWA, CS, Chartered Accountant, Institute of Costs Accountants of India and Company Secretary.

Please bear with me now because the path to a gold mine is always very hard.

Basically, you have to be an accountant wearing expensive suits to be on the panel of IBC, Insolvency and Bankruptcy Code, 2016.

That is where the Vijay Mallya-type of cases land where there are thousands of crores rupees worth of assets and the RP decides their fate along with the COC, nothing to do with the good morning, cock-a-doodle-doo cock.

This COC is committee of creditors which are mainly government-owned banks. Together the RP and COC agree how the insolvency case should be resolved and they put their seasoned views before IBBI, Insolvency and Bankruptcy Board of India, where very learned men and women pass judgement on 'haircuts', taking into account 'commercial wisdom' of the RP and the COC.

Just as an aside, nothing could be recovered from Vijay Mallya because he only left his Kingfisher calendars and 'King of Good Times' photos behind. Everything else, he took with him. But not all other failed businesses are as lucky.

AIBEA, oh so sorry, I mean All India Bank Employees Association came up with a list of 10 insolvent businesses. The COC, or banks that lent money, said they were owed 61,832 crore rupees ($7.4 billion) from 10 companies that went bankrupt.

Ten *Adani* group companies bought these through proper IBC and IBBI procedure at 15,977 crore rupees ($1.9 billion, a discount of 74% over the claim amount.

The state-owned banks got their heads shaved bald at Lucky Hair Cut Saloon at Bail Bazar, Kurla, and the RP, or several RPs are probably having a martini in Paris, shaken not stirred.

If any of you super-brainy IIT, IIM boys and girls want a further lesson from me after 7 p.m, please take an appointment and BYOB.

Words decoded:

Adani :   The family name of Gautam, a businessman very close
           to Prime Minister Narendra Modi and said to be
           benefiting hugely from that connection.

On November 21, 2024, Gautam Adani was charged by the U.S. Department of Justice of paying bribes of $265 million to Indian government officials to secure solar energy supply contracts.

9

A CONFESSION TO MAKE

After having given very good career advice to our nation's kids with an Intelligence Quotient of 200 and above, I must make a confession.

Just for context the world's largest and most respected organisation that gives tests and certifies prodigies in IQ matters is called Mensa and members of this distinguished body go on to head companies like Apple and Microsoft at an annual pay of $100 million and stocks grants of another $900 million.

With an IQ of around 50, my career choices were limited and that was not such a bad thing at all. There was no agonising and fretting over whether I should become a doctor or an engineer.

In 1975, when I passed my 10th board examination life was uncomplicated. If you were a Mensa-type topper and got 80% and above, you had to go for science and study to become a doctor or an engineer. If you dared do anything else, you were excommunicated.

If you got between 45% and 60%, you were put in a cattle pound to get a degree in commerce with dreams that you would then get that coveted chartered accounting certificate. If you failed in that subsequent step, you made repeated applications and appeared for multiple tests to become a probationary officer at State Bank of India, which was not bad at all.

The pay was decent, promotion prospects were healthy and more importantly owing to it being a secure government job, your prospects in the matrimonial market rose substantially.

At St. Anthonys High School in the aforementioned Vakola I was summoned by the good-natured Father Allwyn D'Silva to ask what stream of study I would like to choose. Unsure of what to say because I had never ever given it any thought before, I said hesitantly, Eh Science?

Father Allwyn sympathetically shook his head twice, left to right and once again in the same sequence. Commerce? I suggested and Father Allwyn poked me on the shoulder and said "You go do Arts".

Those days all boys who did Arts were considered Farts but I never held it against Father Allwyn because with a 37% pass average, I was thankful he at least let me get in there. God bless Father Allwyn, who is now an auxiliary bishop at the Archdiocese of Bombay.

That academic year was the most pleasant because I was one among six boys amid 40 pretty girls. The daily proceedings were not too taxing either, studying history of the Mohenjo-daro civilisation and remembering the angle at which the earth's axis stood.

That also meant even pleasanter nights because when my mates pored over tomes of physics, biology, chemistry and how to balance books of accounts, I practised how to balance a book on my index finger while twirling it round and round.

It made us all feel very hungry and just past midnight at the vacant flat of a relative where we went to burn the midnight oil, much to the misplaced delight of our concerned parents, one of the studious types would suggest that I be despatched on my bicycle to go get *pav* bhaji.

None of us had the money to fund such an acquisition and with banks closed at that hour, chances of a loan too were limited. So, we looked up to Sandeep who always had money, and he generously handed it out after his hunger overtook his rationality.

Now those were pre-plastic-bag days and if you went to buy anything you had to take along your own cloth bag, called 'pishvi' in Marathi. It was a simple thing - two pieces of cloth measuring 10 inches by 16 inches stitched together on three sides by dear mother at home on her Singer sewing machine.

On the unstitched open part on top, she put two little triple folded and stitched horseshoe shaped cuffs to hold the pishvi or to hang it by a cycle handlebar. Problem was we could not take the cloth bag from home because dear *Ama* would want to know why we needed a pishvi at night.

My brother Bhaskar Khandeparkar, who was studying architecture and was in the habit of using as a pillow a fat book titled 'History of Global Architecture by Sir Banister Fletcher' came up with what later got known as the 'pyjama plan'.

It was what might be called 'out-of-the box thinking'. He asked me to change into my short pants, took the pyjama I was wearing, turned it upside down and tied knots toward the end of each leg.

"This side is to put the bhaji and this other side is to put the pav and *kanda-limbu* marke," he said holding it by the string, or naada, as we called it. Once the twin pishvi was full and you held the naada end up, it would shut like an automatic ziplock bag.

So, as you can see my five years from age 16 to 20, two years of junior college and three years of senior college went by like a dream. What I did not realise then was that it would totally destroy my score on the marriage market.

My family is Brahmin, to be specific Konkani-speaking *Gaud Saraswat Brahmin*, and generally considered very strong in the doctors and engineers department. When word got around to prospective fathers-in-law that yet another 'promising' GSB boy had just passed out, I started getting calls.

Such news was then made viral at family events like weddings, extremely noisy. This Mr. Shenoy, Kamath, or Pai, I can't recall, was told I had just passed out with a BA, Bachelor of Arts, degree.

Amid the shehnai flute and drums, the old man just retired from State Bank of India, mistook it for BE, Bachelor of Engineering, and called me on phone most respectfully. He delicately said to me that I would make a good husband for his daughter and wanted to know my current daily pursuit.

I said I have no job yet and he said, "Oh that's okay, you will get one soon. So, what are you, mechanical, electrical, chemical?" Engineer, he meant.

It was painful but I had to clarify that BE is not what I had in hand but BA. Faster than the speed of sound he cut the call and I slowly put the handset of my MTNL, *Mahanagar* Telephone *Nigam* Limited, phone back on the cradle.

Words decoded:

Pav bhaji	: A Mumbai-invented mixed vegetable mashed on a large iron pan, served with lime-squeezed finely-chopped raw onion and bread.
Kanda	: Onion
Limbu	: Lime
Marke	: Beat the shit out of it
Kanda-nimbu marke	: You get the drift, right!
Ama	: Mother, mostly South Indian
Mahanagar	: Big city
Nigam	: Corporation
Mahanagar Telephone Nigam Limited	: Big City Telephone Corporation Limited
Gaud	: Name of a kingdom by that name in Bengal
Saraswat	: Those who lived on the banks of river Saraswati that originated in the Himalayas and was central to ancient Indian civilisation. The river dried up thousands of years ago, forcing those who lived on its bank to migrate to Gauda in Bengal.

Gaud Saraswat
Brahmin : Shortened to GSB, the people who lived in the Kashmir valley, where river Saraswati after flowing down from the Himalayas, had its first point of contact with humans. From Bengal, the GSB's later moved to Gujarat, then Goa and some moved further down to Karnataka.

The St. Anthony's School buildings draped in blue, stand on either side of St. Anthony's church in Vakola of Santacruz in Mumbai. The school buildings' and students' uniforms used to be a combination of beige and brown then. Now, it is blue and we do not know why.

10

AMITABH BACHCHAN

My prospective father-in-law's rudeness did not affect me at all, and life went on for me as usual, dashing here and there on my bicycle, and going to watch 9 p.m to 12 midnight movies with my friend Tony Pinheiro from *Vijay* Kunj housing society.

Kunj, meaning a place full of creepers or clinging plants, used to be a very popular prefix or suffix to housing society names in the seventies. We had a Vijay Kunj and a Kunj *Vihar* too in Vakola.

Most of the movies I went to see were Amitabh Bachchan's famous pictures like *Deewar*, *Zanzeer* and *Don*. We all admired him very much and so it was a substantial shock when much later, in year 2001 to be precise, I came face-to-face with the superstar. Actually, it was more side-face to side-face.

Amitabh was at the men's urinal pots at the Maurya Sheraton luxury hotel in Delhi, pissing.

I was doing the same, right next to him, both holding our hands below with great care to aim properly.

Just after the first pressure eased off, I turned to my left, saw Amitabh and was so awestruck that if I wasn't holding on to a more important job then, I might have extended my hand to shake his hand.

It was all too short, all of it lasting less than a minute, and then Mr. Bachchan went striding away majestically. I ambled out shortly, too dazed.

Later, much later, I thought: "Maybe, I should have said 'Hello' and struck up a conversation." It is very difficult to start talk with a superstar at such times and hold it up properly for too long in a loo.

I was then a month-long-stay resident at the Maurya Sheraton, which is the time an international news company allots you at an expensive hotel after a new posting until you select your company-paid apartment, which again is not permanent, but lasts for three years or so, until you are posted out to another place.

I was there soon after the millennium, Year 2000, to hire and manage 22 new people for a news desk to hyper-loop Reuters into the post Y2K Internet and Online news world. That Reuters venture failed with the dot-com bust two years later.

But I still maintain that calm poise, pissing in public places, though I know that Amitabh Bachchan moment will never come back again.

Words decoded:

Vijay : Victory

Vihar : A place to rest and meditate

Deewar : Wall

Zanjeer : A heavy iron chain

Don : Gangster, opposite of Don Bosco and same as Don Corleone

Amitabh Bachchan on the sets of one of his movies in the eighties when he was all the rage in Bollywood

11

LONDON AND THE
ELEPHANT TRUNK PICKLE

That assignment as Online Editor for India was the last one I had at Reuters because in an unprecedented show of brilliance, the company's Asian editorial management at that time somehow arrived at the conclusion that the global dot-com bust was all my fault and they fired me.

I moved on to Dow Jones Newswires after that, then Bloomberg News as an editor on the Asian energy desk and finally as a columnist for the Wall Street Journal, but my decade-long tenure with Reuters remains the most memorable because the company gave me the opportunity to train in London, work in Manila, Mumbai and Delhi and sent me on multiple expensive refresher courses in Hong Kong and Singapore.

To two people, I owe much for my happy days at Reuters and for imparting to me skills that stood me well later when I could walk at will into writing or editing jobs in any international media company of my choice. One of them was George Short, Reuters' legendary training editor.

After Short died in June 1997 Andrew Gumbel, now an author based in Los Angeles, wrote this for British paper, Independent:

"Short could have taught an armchair to write well-turned, simple prose, he also had a warm, generous personality and a sharp wit that made his students adore every minute they spent with him. Here he was, a great cuddly bear of a man, cracking jokes in his purring Devon accent, telling elaborate anecdotes about his colleagues or recalling past drinking binges; he seemed at odds with the dry, competitive world of news-agency journalism. Yet he put heart and soul into his work, his commitment to professional standards unwavering".

Outside class, I met Short sometimes at a Pret a Mongrel, or some such sandwich shop, where I stopped by to pick my lunch to have on the nice grounds of St. Brides Church on Fleet Street.

George would ask what I was buying for lunch and seeing on the counter a very tall jar of marinated stuff floating in an off-white fluid, I often said: "I am having this elephant trunk pickle. It is good; you should have it too."

The second person to who I owe gratitude is Jeremy Clift who as bureau chief for Reuters in Mumbai hired me and taught me real journalism, mostly in the fierce heat of the newsroom when your work is measured in seconds because you are feeding realtime news to trading rooms that bet millions on what you put out that very instant.

Clift later moved on to management, becoming country head for Reuters in Jakarta and later still as head of publications for the International Monetary Fund in Washington. Nowadays my mentor mostly spends his time on the moon - ever since he wrote this super-seller Sci-fi booked titled 'Born in Space: Unlocking Destiny.'

It is a gripping story of a booming lunar mining economy where sinister American billionaires hijack in mid-space asteroids with precious minerals that are being tugged back to base by good people with good intent. It has a funny human touch too with earthlings yearning for their own lunar radio station that will give them a bright start each day with the radio host saying a cheery: 'Good Morning, Lunatics".

Clift's book won first place in the Sci-if series category at the Los-Angeles-based Book Fest Awards for 2024.

Central London, where in places such as Fleet Street the biggest newspapers and news agencies had their offices. Now, media companies can no more afford to stay in posh enclaves which have been taken over by global banks and the Donald Trump types

12

LUNATICS ON EARTH TOO

I feel very much at home in Clift's fascinating inter-galactic world because I now live among lunatics, not all the time but during some phases. I mean I live in the same place all the time with nice and sane people who turn crazy some specific months of the year at the most unexpected of times, like the annual Ganapati festival that is most auspicious and happy.

Ganapati is close to my heart as growing up we had dozens of idols at home, not necessarily for worshipping but as symbols of quiet divine adoration. Ganapati is my family's *kula devta*, designated chief God of our clan, and we are trustees of the Mahaganapati Temple in Khandola, Goa that has its origins in the 16th century.

And so it was odd that one evening in 2023, I felt Ganapati throbbing in a very noisy and unhealthy manner when the big community idols were being taken for a ceremonial immersion in the sea.

It was all quite indistinct from my side of the road and I had to cross over to the other side. Just in case you think how can you not know what is happening right across your street, here's the context. I live on GMLR, which is Goregaon Mulund Link Road, that has six lanes full of murderous motorists driving West to East and on the other side of the divider another eight lanes of maniacs steering hard East to West.

It takes quite a bit of tact, divine support, and courage to cross over but it is worth it to be witness to a haze of dust and a maze of a hundred hands multiplied by 100 gyrating wildly in the air to strobe lights - red, blue, red, saffron, and searing hot white.

And they are all dancing wildly to a Bollywood song that goes: Ae jee, oh jee, lo jee, suno jee... *one two ka four, four two ka one ...* my name is Lakhan, my name is Lakhan!

And then I see Ganapati in the truck ahead facing backward and as I say a silent prayer the Lord, he asks me: "Who is Lakhan? I don't know Bappa," I say. Maybe a mathematician because they said: "One two ka four" which is a very complex thing.

The street sides smell of urine and the together-struggling body mass emit stale sweat through their synthetic-saffron shirts sponsored by Hindutva heroism-type political parties. But it's not all that bad because if anyone is on the verge of a heart attack, free CPR, cardio-pulmonary resuscitation comes from the strong thumping of your chest by 10,000 watts of bass that is by now playing:

"Aarey Diwano, Mujhe Pechano; Kaha'n se aaya, Mai hoo'n kaun?

Mai hoo'n kaun, mai hoo'n kaun???

Mai hoo'n, mai hoo'n mai hoo'n Don... Don, Don, Don!

Words decoded:

Kula   :   Clan

Devta   :   Deity

Bappa Morya   :   A reverential suffix to Ganapati

Ae jee, oh jee, lo jee, suno jee...; one two ka four, four two ka one, my name is Lakhan: Gee, so many of us here – me, you, she too, hearing me sing one plus two make four; four plus two make one and my name is Lakhan.

Arre Diwano, mujhe pechano ...: Crazy dudes, you know me? Who am I? Tell me. I am, Don you stupid. This song is from the movie Don referred to in chapter 10.

Sorry to break protocol but at this stage after being hearing Lakhan and Don's songs, I feel like screaming 'Aata majhi satakli', the meaning of which you will find in words decoded, chapter 3.

Ganapati is a God much revered and loved across India and is the object of sincere devotion as seen in this picture on a sandy beach just before the idols are immersed into the sea.

It is the big community -Ganapati celebrations, funded by political parties, that have perverted the festival.

13

IF YOU IGNORE THIS ABERRATION, GANAPATI WENT GREEN A LONG TIME AGO

In my family in Goa, the Ganapati brought home for Chaturthi was never of plaster of Paris with chemical colours and it wasn't clay either. The idol was made of papier mache, a tradition that has gone on for centuries, and now applauded by green activists saying: "Oh so cool! These Khandeparkars' were well ahead of their time".

Thank You, Thank You, but the real reason is different. Our ancestral temple was originally located on the island of Diwar. That was among the first territories the Portuguese conquered in 1510, and the first 50 years were benign.

But by 1560, the Catholic Inquisition, a judicial system of the Church that persecuted and punished people who did not follow Christianity arrived in Goa and started destroying Hindu temples and the idols within.

The old stone idols were too heavy to run away with in the face of European artillery and after facing many losses, my ancestors in the quiet of one night took the original Ganapati into the jungles of Ponda, outside Portuguese authority and that original 16th-century idol still sits at the family temple in Khandola.

But for daily worship, they used the sketch of Ganapati on paper - easy to roll, tuck under your arm and go to safety with your God along with you in times of danger. And that paper Ganapati tradition in my family continues to this day.

After the earlier vicious period, Portugal changed as the winds of democracy swept over Lisbon, it turned tolerant and left behind good things that exist to this day. Goa is the only state in India to have a Uniform Civil Code and is the only province that recognises the rights of the original clans over their temple properties and trusts under what was called the Regulamento das Mazanias Act, 1933.

Our families, the trustees of all Hindu temples in Goa, are called Mhajan, shortened from the Portuguese Mazanias.

14

VIVA PORTUGAL

That is why Goans of my vintage have a fondness for the Portuguese, for the archives they left behind and the exotic fusion of culture, food, and wine, which has over the years got promoted to whisky, not for vice but purely cultural upbringing reasons.

Try as hard as the Portuguese did, the new converts to Christianity quickly reverted to old Hindu customs, especially when they attended events with extended family who stayed Hindu. So, the church on orders from Lisbon produced a plan that would ostracise the newly converted Christians from their former faith-mates.

"Make them eat beef and pork," they said. That way the newly named Michael, formerly Mahadev, would never again be accepted by his old clan. There was one big problem - Mahadev Michael was so revulsed by the thought, smell and taste of beef and pork that he just could not swallow it.

The Portuguese said: "Get them to drink - so their inhibitions disappear", and it was peddled as part of normal life - "Have lots of feni - eat meat and sleep well". And liquor was made available at every turn on the road and very cheap too by the crafty Portuguese.

Our Gaud Saraswat Brahman, even more crafty, did some logical deduction and arrived at his own happy conclusion that since Hinduism did not explicitly disapprove of a drink, unlike beef and pork, they could regularly have a few as long as they stuck to Bangdya hooman, a spicy mackerel fish curry had with rice.

And so it is - alcohol is not so much taboo in Goan GSB homes. In theory we still don't touch pork sorpotel and beef vindaloo and on austere Mondays, we don't have bangdya hooman either, only *tambdi bhaji*, but drink we do - it is allowed.

Words decoded:

Tambdi   :   Red

Bhaji   :   Vegetable

Tambdi bhaji :   Amaranth, a red leafy vegetable

15

YOU CAN USE COCONUT HAIR OIL BUT NO COCONUTS ON A PLANE

Just to clarify, not all GSB, Gaud Saraswat Brahman are of the 'folga maruya' type, which is Goan Konkani for, "Let's just chill, dude".

There are those from Mangalore, like my very conservative mother Mukta Kashinath Khandeparkar, who was brought up in a very healthy coastal life where coconuts were aplenty. So that defined everything from what I ate, coconut-based fish curries and vegetables and coconut oil rubbed liberally into my hair.

That is why, I was shocked when I read that advanced airport security in India by the lean and mean men and women of the CISF, Central Industrial Security Force, will not allow coconuts in hand baggage.

Airport security is very important, and I understand the difficulties the enforcers face - like any permissible liquid more than 100 ml is not allowed on board.

Now a coconut has water inside and there is no way airport police by shaking a nut near the ear can determine if the liquid inside is less than 100 ml, or more. You may think of breaking the coconut just before the bomb detector, drink a bit and offer some to co-flyers as 'tirth', holy water. Coconut is a sacred fruit in India and is offered in temples to God.

But airport manual says two broken half-nuts are not allowed either because they have lots of oil and are highly inflammable.

In my infant days when my mother slathered my head with this good stuff, I never heard airport security saying to her: "Hey, not allowed. Your boy is flammable because he has too much coconut oil on his head".

Because we never flew then. Could not afford it so we went by Ghatge Patil bus - Sion to Hampankatta, Mangalore and Rorex Travels' jolly coach, Dhobi Talao to Panaji, Goa.

16

GOAN *SUSEGAD* VERSUS MANGALOREAN STAUNCHNESS

My mother's side of the family is very conservative and a lot more focused. Called 'Amchigele', meaning our people, I think. They are far more disciplined than the Goan Gaud Saraswat Brahman and far more successful, in career, business or religious rituals. Like the GSB *Seva Mandal* whose five-day annual Ganapati festival is by far the richest such organisation.

Until the seventies, Mangalorean GSB's more than matched the *Shetty* community in running *idli-dosa* restaurants in Mumbai, but over the years the *Bunts* went far ahead because they were practical and moved on to bars selling Indian whisky by the bottle at near MRP, maximum retail price, and served the freshest of fish dishes, topped with shredded coconut on top.

The Konkani-speaking Mangalorean GSB may drink the finest of Scotch outside of home to go with Chicken 65, but at home and at workplace, never. Eventually, the Tulu-speaking Bunt practicality ran the Amchigele puritans out of the restaurant business.

Very few of the old iconic GSB-owned restaurants minus Officers Choice Whisky, Old Monk Rum and Chicken 65 are still alive and one of them is Cafe Mysore at Kings Circle, owned by my sister Shanteri Nayak, who was greeted by Anant Ambani and his bride Radhika at their wedding by bowing low, hand on their hearts. That video of the billionaire couple displaying utmost humility and saying how much they enjoyed her restaurant food that they ate every Sunday went viral.

Anant's father Mukesh Ambani studied chemical engineering at UDCT, University Department of Chemical Engineering, walking distance from Cafe Mysore and his fondness for that simple food from those days in the seventies, extends to this day.

Every weekend, Cafe Mysore's old delights go take-away to the Ambani household and often is ordered for serving on Reliance's private planes.

A. Rama Nayak took control of Cafe Mysore in 1958 along with a clutch of other restaurants and bequeathed them to each of his sons before he passed on. Cafe Mysore went to Nagesh, his eldest son, a top-notch electrical engineer by training with more interest in technology than idlis. Had he moved on to the U.S, he would have been a Silicon Valley billionaire.

But family values prevailed and Nagesh, my brother-in-law, stayed on to innovate ways of managing a steeped-in-tradition business while retaining the original food flavours.

In the late 1970s, when other Udipi restaurant owners never ever left the cash counter because of possible pilferage, Nagesh left the money handling to his staff and those were days when it was your 100% turnover. No cards to swipe and no GPay.

At a time when software programmes were not available to monitor order flow and cash flow, Nagesh set himself free to focus on quality rather than sit all day long with his hands dipped in steel *vatis* full of coins.

How he did this was utterly simple and butterly brilliant. In the kitchen, he ordered shiny new stainless-steel drums in which the *urad dal, tuvar dal, rice, moong* and other essentials were placed. On the inside of each drum, he got engraved lines showing every two-kilo capacity. If the day started with 24 kilos, he knew exactly for every drop in the level how many dosas and idlis were made, give or take a few.

If the cash collection did not match the levels in the drum, he knew someone had put his hand in the till. Nagesh focussed on the bigger aspects of Cafe Mysore like getting away from the sub-lease system that his father had started with in the heritage building that it is still located in prominently at Kings Circle.

Nagesh got admission at the prestigious IIT in Madras for civil engineering but decided not to take it because his father A. Rama Nayak wanted him to be nearer home to help run the four restaurants he owned. He went to VJTI, Victoria Jubilee Technical Institute, in Matunga to study electrical engineering.

To support his family, Nagesh stayed a Matunga man all his life; went to Don Bosco School, Ramniranjan Ruia College, VJTI and Café Mysore, all in Matunga. His commitment and talent did not go waste.

Nagesh, who died young in 2009, secured the entire building for the restaurant and today Café Mysore's kitchens are spread over two floors, giving their cooks the space needed to continue creating *sambhar* and chutney magic. He worked systematically to get near 100 percent control of the building which was under the so-called pagdi system.

Pagdi was a sensible market response to World War Two, when colonial ruler Britain, extensively used Indian soldiers to fight for them. That required commandeering houses to station all the troops at main hubs, before the Indian boys were flown out to die in a battle in Europe that they knew nothing about.

The commandeering or forced take over of private properties by the British army caused a housing shortfall and led to a big rise in rental prices. To keep a check on this, the British came up with a Rent Control Act, which with typical Indian ingenuity was kept on the statute books by our lawmakers much after the English people left.

That Rent Control Act kept rents as low as 25 rupees, when demand-supply said it was 200 rupees. It started off a market-determined offset mechanism where to transfer the property, the land and building owner demanded an upfront deposit of say 5,000 rupees. That deposit, or pagdi, was shared between the seller tenant and landowner.

To get each of the tenements in the Café Mysore building transferred to himself, Nagesh paid the pagdi one at a time and eventually came into physical possession of such a substantial part of the valuable structure that the original owner copped out upon some payment he thought fit.

That is why Café Mysore is the only Udipi restaurant in Mumbai that owns the entire building where it is situated. In pricey real estate Mumbai, most other restaurants have an 80:20 ratio, 80% for guest seating and 20% for the kitchen. In Café Mysore, it is the reverse, I think!

It allows their chefs the space to create chutney and sambar magic. Naresh Nayak, Nagesh's son, who now runs the restaurant will know the exact kitchen to seating ratio, just as his mother knows the exact hourly schedule of fresh chutney's made for each meal session.

Chutney from the earlier session is never passed on to the next. Always fresh! That is why Mukesh Ambani swears by it.

Words decoded:

Seva   : Public service

Mandal   : Refer chapter 5 on Navaratri

Shetty   : A very common surname of a highly entrepreneurial community in Karnataka state

Bunt   : The caste to which Shetty people belong

Vati   : A small steel bowl to have chutney that also doubles up as a receptacle for restaurant owners to put in coins that they earn from selling chutney

Tur dal   : Yellow lentil

Urad dal   : Black lentil

Moong dal : A lentil of confused identity – when wet it looks green and dried looks yellow

Sambhar   : Tasty tur dal-based Apple phone accessory to have with idli. Now do not ask me what idli is, please!

Cafe Mysore, Mumbai's famous South Indian vegetarian restaurant, that is now run by Naresh, the third generation of the Nayak family. They serve 100-year-old dishes like 'khotto', which is idli batter steamed in the leaves of a jackfruit tree, said to be very healthy.

17

WRONG PERSPECTIVES FROM THE 1980S CORRECTED NOW

Café Mysore and the Ambani family's 50-year-long patronage of Café Mysore brings me to their patriarch, the late Dhirubhai, who was a gas station attendant in Aden in Yemen before returning to India to lay the foundation of one of India's biggest and most successful conglomerates.

Sometime mid-eighties, Dhirubhai Ambani wanted to build a world-class polyester filament yarn factory, and the machinery was not available in India. He wanted to import the entire plant, but the government of the day had a ridiculous 400% customs duty on it.

There is a background to this in that the local textile mill owners then were rich and powerful and they did not want cheaper and longer-lasting foreign fabric to destroy their captive business.

Dhirubhai saw through this and decided he would make the fabric in India but the 400% import duty made it unviable.

Dhirubhai looked at the customs law book and found out that while import duty on an entire polyester plant was 400 percent, it was only 25% on components for the plant. Our bureaucrats must have kept duty on components at a much lower 25% thinking if there was no such factory at all in India, why would anyone want its components. Dhirubhai imported each element and nut bolt of an entire plant at different ports in India and then assembled it all together in one factory.

Was Dhirubhai wrong and did he deprive the Indian government of legitimate revenue. No! He was right because if you have a stupid government that imposes a 400% percent penalty on somebody working hard for his dream, the problem lies with the state and its rulers.

Dhirubhai worked the *license-raj* barriers to get face time with those that mattered. Reliance had the first-row VIP seat booked everyday on the morning Indian Airlines flight Bombay to Delhi. Most days the money went waste, but somedays airline staffers would tip off about a politician or big bureaucrat travelling and a Reliance man would show up in the seat next, getting two hours of unhindered time.

Words decoded:

License   : Permit

Raj   : Unbridled power

License Raj : Socialist India's governance system until the 1991 economic liberalisation and since independence in 1947 under which the government decided which business house would produce what, in what quantum, or not manufacture at all because foolish Indians had to be saved from useless goods. It was patriotism, totally misplaced. Former Prime Minister Manmohan Singh, who died on December 26, 2024 dismantled the License Raj and ushered an economic liberalisation as Finance Minister in 1991.

18

BOMBAY PROHIBITION ACT, 1949 AND OTHER DELUSIONS OF THIS CITY

License-raj reminded me that the Bombay Prohibition Act, 1949 is still in force in Mumbai city and Maharashtra state. This dates back to days of British rule over India when administrative districts were called 'presidency' and the Bombay presidency included what are now the states of Maharashtra and Gujarat.

Indian states were reorganised in 1960 along linguistic lines ands since then much water, or more appropriately alcohol, has flown under the bridges of Bombay. But the Bombay Prohibition Act, 1949 has not yet been revoked because it gives license to politicians and law enforcement agencies to take high moral ground whenever they run out of cash to collar a harassed office worker having a quiet drink saying: "Hey, where is your permit, your liquor permit".

Legally, it is a crime to drink alcohol in Maharashtra without a permit but practically it is all fine because everyone who matters is paid off monthly not to ask about this permit. Now, owing to this many of our younger generation are not even aware that there exists such a permit.

I have one and mine is a lifetime permit that has an official government logo with my picture, my address and a full disclosure in Marathi, which I have translated for your benefit: It says: "Uday Khandeparkar is legally entitled under Bombay Prohibition Act, 1949, and related rules in Maharashtra state to buy alcohol of the English and country varieties, to have in possession and consume strictly for himself only".

This Act came into effect 11 years before I was born in 1960 and still stays on our legal books when I am 64 years old, but I don't mind it at all. I really like it.

It is a very handy wallet-protecting weapon to wield because when friends ask me to buy them a drink, I say: "Look, my government permit allows only me to drink for life, Okay! If I give you a drink, I will be put in jail".

I can't vouch for this, but I am told such Bombay liquor permits earlier required you to have a doctor certify that you needed to have a few small ones every day because your medical condition required you to. Imagine a white-coated doctor's prescription saying, "Rx Please take 'one stiff before lunch and three strong ones before dinner".

Bombay, now Mumbai, is so much fun in the department of delusions. Like everyone, especially Maharashtra politicians, cling to Mumbai because it is by far India's richest city. It is true that Mumbai is India's wealthiest enclave with a GDP of $310 billion, but that does not mean the wealth is generated here.

The wealth generation is happening in Jamnagar, Gujarat, where the world's single-location largest refinery is, owned by Reliance Industries; the income generation and real production is happening in Jamshedpur at the Tata Steel factory in Jharkhand, at the Tata Motors factory in Pimpri-Chinchwad and for the Aditya Birla group the biggest plants are in Uttar Pradesh and Madhya Pradesh.

It just so happens that the registered offices of India's biggest companies happen to be in Mumbai and so do their billionaire owners for historic reasons and the corporate and personal income taxes are all paid in this city.

Mumbai's real contribution to GDP is *vada pav*, ad film makers, Bollywood and the expensive real estate that supports this mirage. So sorry to burst your Bombay balloon, Uddhavji and Shinde-saheb.

Words decoded:

Vada   : Steamed and spiced mashed potatoes dipped in chickpea batter and deep fried

Pav   : Bombay bread

Vada Pav : Mumbai burger with the two items listed above plus a garlicky red chilli powder and a hotter-still green chilly marinated and heat-dried next to the cauldron of oil out of which vadas are born.

19

ABSTINENCE AND HYPOCRISY

My family on both Goan and Mangalorean sides, can be very sticky in the optics of how it all looks to others around. They all thoroughly enjoy their drinks and their Chickens 65 privately, but in public most of them will abstain.

Nothing wrong in it because my GSB brothers and sisters follow the Gujarati hypocrisy where prohibition is in force because it is the home state of Mahatma Gandhi. As a reporter for the Times of India many decades ago on a junket to Surat, I saw the Gujarati brain come up with a most innovative solution to what is prohibited by law - serving alcohol.

At a pool-side party at a friendly hotel, much before the press party arrived, in front of each of the six chairs around multiple round tables were placed full 750 ml bottles of a then popular brand of Indian whisky.

I found it very odd then but after having a few, my brain sparked, and I realised that the hosts were protecting themselves from the long arm of the law. In case any khaki-uniformed enforcer of virtue walked in, I suppose they would simply say, "Officer, see we are not serving them any alcohol, they came with their own bottles and are also pouring it themselves."

Fortunately, that evening it did not show up, the long arm of the law I mean, probably because Gujarat those days had the wrong arm of the law. We all must make these minor adjustments like our distinguished diplomats in overseas Indian embassies do.

We have our days of national importance like Republic Day on January 26 and His/ Her Excellency, the Ambassador must host a dinner to fellow diplomats from other nations and important people in the city that the Embassy is located in.

One such patriotic evening, I was at the Republic Day grand party hosted in Manila by the Indian ambassador to the Philippines. I noticed very thin attendance at the dinner as liveried waiters went around passing over to guests' glasses of *jal jeera* and spiced butter milk. Patriotic Indians do not drink alcohol on days patriotic.

Suddenly, between 9:30 p.m. and 9:45 p.m. some two dozen white diplomats, all ruddy-faced and looking very happy trooped in. Since I was working with Reuters then, the press attaché in the British embassy was a friend. I asked her the secret of this collectively timed happy invasion and she said: "Today January 26th, is also Australia Day and you know they serve the best of wines."

At the Indian embassy party, you start off with an uninspiring butter milk, but you fire on all cylinders after eating *galouti kabab, chicken tikka, mutton do-pyaaza with rumali roti, dal makhani and*

dum biryani Kashmir, delicately dum cooked with expensive saffron.
I understood then those diplomats had to be diplomatic.

You can't offend any one country. You go to Australia Day first
and then you go to the Indian Republic Day soiree. I would have
done the same if I was the Australian ambassador in Manila then:
At about 9:15 p.m., I would have said to the guards outside, "Okay
boys, take the Australian flag down for the night and put it back up
tomorrow at 7 a.m," and headed to the Indian embassy party to have
a tandoori chicken.

Words decoded:

Jal   : Water

Jeera   : Cumin

Jal jeera   : Cumin water. It's actually a lot nicer than
just that. It has mint leaves, the extract of
tamarind, black salt, and a light touch of
green chilli

Galauti kebab   : Spiced goat mince roll skewered on a coal
fire. The mince is ground so fine that it
melts in your mouth before you bite it,
which means you can eat it without your
dentures on

Chicken tikka   : A full-sized arrogant chicken tandoori cut
down to size

Mutton do-piazza : Do is two and piaz is onion. Now don't
jump to a conclusion that it is mutton with

two onions only. It is Mr Meat getting married to Ms Onion twice, first when they boil together with all the spices and second when mutton meets her again as tempering, straight from a crackling ladle along with garlic flakes and other aromatic stuff.

Roomali roti : A fine wheat flour bread that is made, not by a chef but by a juggler and magician combined. The dough is meant to be stretched so thin that conventional rolling won't work. So, they launch it up in the air in a circular motion like a frisbee, catch it delicately and launch it up several times more until the roti is like a 1960s woman's veil for church-going Sunday's.

It is roasted on an upturned iron vat and folded neatly like a roomal, which means handkerchief. Hence Roomali.

Dal Makhani : A rich and buttery lentil stew made with urad dal (black lentils) and rajma (red kidney beans). To get that intense flavour, it is cooked by simmering overnight on coal embers, or so they say.

Biryani : If you don't know what biryani is, I give up.

20

ON DEATH AND OBITS

I don't go to high-flying parties anymore because I am of that age where I am losing more friends to death than I am making new ones. Nothing wrong with this, it is natural where the old must make way for the new. What I find funny is people posting on Facebook, saying: "Oh, what a good soul, she was! Referring to the just dead.

Absolute paragon of virtue and my world will never be the same again and all that.

Hello! Until yesterday you said what a pain in the 'B' for brain, she was.

Be honest in your obit comments on me when my time comes, which is still a long way away, I think!

I can help edit some of those for clarity, but sentences like: "Oh! What an Old Fart, Uday was," will not be allowed.

Now, I will go have another whisky and think up good Obit lines for me.

21

BY PERMISSION OF THE *PARMATMA*

Death is of course a very fleeting thought, one second here and gone the next when I have notions that I have been sent here for a larger purpose. It mostly happens when I have had one too much to drink.

In the middle of the dark night when all is dead quiet, a powerful desire to pee wakes me up from a dream in which an angel tells me that God sent me. I am befuddled and after an incomplete prostate-impaired pee go right back to sleep to continue my conversation with Parmatma.

God never comes back but I do dream of me flying in my pyjama and banian over the icy Himalayan ranges, then diving into the Bay of Bengal without pyjama and banian. When I surface, groggily awake, I find myself in bed in Dindoshi of Goregaon in Mumbai.

A little later I go to look for my old copy of 'The Interpretation of Dreams, by Sigmund Freud'. I can't find it and so I ask Google girl, and she tells me that these are rare but real cases - it happened to Idi Amin in 1972 when God told him to kick all Asians, meaning Indians, out of Uganda overnight.

It happened to Narendra Modi too who famously said before the last parliamentary elections in June 2024 that he has a direct connection with parmatma and he was sent to earth by God to serve the people of India.

Like, I think, God must have said to Modi at the peak of Covid in March, 2022 to instruct his people to do solid work and used the proverb 'Empty vessels make more noise' to prove the opposite. God meant be full of substance and work hard to conquer Covid.

These Godly messages come in the dead of the night when our faculties are dimmed by sleep and Modi did what I would have done. "Bhaiyon aur Beheno," he said at 8 p.m. on national television. "Tomorrow, at 8 p.m. bring out all your empty steel pots, aluminium pans and brass plates out in your balconies and bang the hell out of them."

What a visual treat it was to see such simian discipline displayed by millions of my country men and women, though audio-wise the divinity of it all was diluted a bit by babies crying and animals running scared. "What the hell has happened to these humans," my neighbour's collar-less cat said to the collared dog in the verandah opposite.

As you can see, I am part of a very eminent circle and hence I know that divine messages can sometimes come all garbled when Internet connection from heaven to earth is weak. Ordinary mortals such as you dear reader will not understand and here I appropriately quote American actress, comedian and writer Lily Tomlin who said:

"Why is it that when we talk to God, we are said to be praying. But when God talks to us, we are schizophrenic."

Words decoded:

Parmatma	:	Shortened from param atma
Param	:	Eternal
Atma	:	Soul
Param Atma	:	Eternal soul, a very profound thought. For simpler minds, it means God.
Bhaiyon aur behenon	:	My dear brothers and sisters, a favoured first introductory line of Modi's nation-wide speeches that started at 8 p.m and dropped a bombshell saying at 12 midnight, four hours from now, 80% of the currency notes value-wise in your wallet would become invalid.

The same shockingly effective technique was used during Covid when Modi said on national television at 8 p.m. that from 12 midnight, four hours later, it would be "total lockdown Dudes". Meaning if you were with a secret boyfriend and could not make it back home to be in time with your husband before midnight, you continue to stay with clandestine boyfriend until the next State of the Union address at 8 p.m.

22

NARENDRA MODI'S SARPA DOSHA

I think the Parmatma-sent Modi is trying to do his best for my revered Hinduism but is still getting it all very wrong. I think Modi is going through '*Sarpa Dosha*', a difficult planetary configuration in Vedic astrology that causes hardships in life.

Sarpa means serpent and they are represented by *Rahu*, the head of the said reptile, and *Ketu* the severed tail of the snake. I'm not surprised that both Rahu and Ketu, head and tail, are both pissed off after separation and if their bad influence falls upon anyone even remotely, even the brightest would falter. Which is why Modi got the Ram *Mandir* manifesto all wrong, that which was to take him '*char-sau paar*'

Before Sarpa dosha caught Modi, he and the BJP did some right things like ending the dispute from Congress-led times on whether this Vishnu avatar was born in Ayodhya and if there ought to be a temple there to Sri Ram.

I have grown up reading Ramayana starting in Ayodhya and journeying with Ram and Laxman across India to Lanka and back to Ayodhya with Sita - like billions of Hindus have over centuries. No one questions that Ram was born in Ayodhya, like no one questions that Jesus was born in Bethlehem or Prophet Mohammad in Mecca.

So having a temple there was a culmination of the faith of thousands of years but the manner of its inauguration was heretic. I am not a follower of ritual but if you must do it, at least follow it by the book. The January 22, 2024 sarpa dosha-tainted charade was inauspicious for three reasons:

1. It fell in the month of Paush, the 10th month of the Hindu lunar calendar, when auspicious events are forbidden.

2. The temple was inaugurated before construction was 100% done, which is not by prescribed ritual. It's like going into an apartment in a rush with no tap water supply before Bombay Municipal Corporation's Occupation Certificate.

3. It was consecrated by Modi as Prime Minister, which ancient Hindu kings never did. Governance and being commander-in-chief of the army was left to the Raja and religion was the domain of the Raj-Purohit, the kingdom's head priest.

Must have been a signal from divinity that in the first heavy rains after Modi took the Prime Minister's chair for the third time even after not getting a majority vote in Parliament, the Ram temple leaked water from the roof and the approach roads got all flooded.

Sarpa Dosha is not a matter to be taken lightly, and Modi should consult the nation's most acclaimed astrologers, and he should inform us all of each step in this process because, "The nation wants to know". 'The Republic wants to know'.

Words decoded:

Sarpa dosha : A planetary configuration that can cause challenges in life. It is said to be a result of past karma.

Rahu : No connection with Rahu Gandhi. It is something ascending on the North Pole and when it is not feeling okay in relation to you, it can cause major effects on your personal life with traits of dishonesty coming to the fore.

Ketu : Something descending on the South Pole

Char : Four

Sau : Hundred

Paar : Cross

Char Sau Paar : Modi's boast in 2024 pre-election campaigning that he would secure for his Bharatiya Janata Party more than 400 seats in the lower house comprising 543, meaning he would completely sweep the polls and cast Rahu into the dustbin. He ended up with just 240, requiring him to take the support of two other regional parties, whose leaders he had called charlatans and thieves in the past.

Rahu : Short for Rahul Gandhi, who Modi considers is a real curse in the path of his emperor glory.

23

MODI'S VISION IS SO FAR AND FAR-FETCHED, YOU NEED A TELESCOPE TO LOOK AT IT

Regardless of Modi's other weaknesses or strengths, one thing he is simply superlative at is making staggeringly grandiose announcements. Like in 2022, when his Finance Minister Nirmala Sitharaman rose in parliament, she presented a big-bang budget with a rocking 35% increase on capital expenditure to build 16 new airports, 200,000 km of world class highways, ultra-modern logistics hubs with multi-modal connectivity to waterways and railways and green energy to fire it all.

The Finance Minister described it as a budget to prepare India for 25 years ahead when we will celebrate the centenary of our independence. And there lies the rub for it means we the people, have to look into a high-powered telescope and feel happy about our advanced nation in Year 2047.

The flip side is that we ignore the near term, such as spiralling prices of essentials, no earnings because of a lack of jobs and no hope in sight either, which would have come in the form of tax breaks to put more money in peoples' pockets.

People spending that money would spur private companies to increase production, hire more people and the virtuous cycle would start almost immediately. The same will happen with the government's massive capital expenditure, except that the trickle-down effect could take years and not manifest in equal measure.

This is because state-run projects leak cash the wrong way despite bad efforts at the top to ensure zero-corruption governance and a bigger risk is that implementation will get delayed or not take off at all. Which would take away the advantage of a bold infra-push that would eventually make our economy more efficient and have a multiplier effect. But let us not be pessimistic.

If we cannot eat bread, or khari biscuit now, we can in Year 2047 eat cake at our world-class airports at Meerut and Bareilly and quaff a few beers at an American diner at Kolhapur as we drive from Kashmir to Kanyakumari on an expressway good enough for planes to take-off.

Until then, keep looking through your telescope and stay content with Modi's upbeat slogans such as 'Make in India'; '*Sabka Sath, Sabka Vikas*' and the most hilarious of them all, '*Acche Din*'.

Words decoded:

Sabka Sath	: All together
Sabka Vikas	: Progress together
Acche	: Better
Din	: Days
Acche Din	: Better days, a promise Modi made before the 2014 elections which won him the prime minister's post for the first time. Ten years later, people are still peering through their miniature version of the Hubble Space Telescope for that elusive star called 'Acche Din'.

Note – in the November, 2024 elections to the Maharashtra state legislature, Modi's party dropped Sabka Sath, Sabka Vikas' and instead came out with 'Batenge toh Katenge'

Toh	: If
Batenge	: Divided
Katenge	: Get slaughtered
Batenge toh katenge	: If you Hindus get divided, the Muslims will slaughter you

24

THE MODI MONETISATION PLAN THAT WAS TO RAISE A 6 FOLLOWED BY 12 ZEROES

The previous year 2021 Modi's government announced a so-called 'Monetisation Plan' that would raise six trillion rupees over four years in a magic move that would pull India out of slush and make it flush - with cash.

These are truly galactic proportions, and the numbers are easier counted in space terms rather than our out of depth *lakhs* and *crores*. One light year is about 6 trillion miles - that is a 6 with 12 zeroes behind it. Like this 6,00,00,00,00,00,00.

Brings to mind a meme of Finance Minister Nirmala Sitharaman leaning close to the ear of Narendra Modi, asking if she could add a few more zeroes and the Prime Minister says: "Add as many zeroes you want. It is just an announcement".

These hopeless pessimists drawing joy out of their stupid memes going viral will know when four years later the Wall Street Journal will have a headline saying: "India zooms into space; America and China fall back to earth."

It is a good plan, this asset monetisation, because it is 'Atmanirbhar', yet another Modi slogan. It is not privatisation or slump sale of state assets. The ownership will stay with the people of India while bringing in cash upfront for the government to build hyper loop that will send people gently hurling down a vacuum tube from Mumbai to Pune in 25 minutes, world class roads, bridges, ports.

It will generate employment for a few lakh crore people and energise private companies into huge capital expenditure to increase capacity to make steel, cement, nuts, bolts, screwdrivers, springs, and big bus-sized vacuum tubes to supply to the government's infrastructure plan.

All this while the monetised assets - roads, gas pipelines, ports, railways and stadiums, languishing now under government mismanagement, will be turned super-efficient by private entrepreneurs.

Just two teeny weeny problems, nothing serious!

1. Super-efficient private chaps may find it difficult to come up with six and 12 zeroes

2. The money may not be spent on new projects but used to cover a fiscal deficit that is now masked off-budget

Don't be a fool and ask then: *"Woh solar-wala bus aur bullet train kaha'n gaya?"* Because *"Woh toh sirf jumla tha!"* Ha, Ha, Ha!!

Words decoded:

Lakh	: 100,000
Crore	: 10 million
Atmanirbhar	: Self reliant
Woh solar-wala bus aur bullet train kaha'n gaya	: So where did the solar-powered bus and a bullet train you promised go?
Woh toh sirf jumla tha	: That was just a lollipop, an imaginary one.

Modi as part of his 'Acche Din' (better days) promise before the 2014 elections had said he would bring back to the country the billions of dollars in slush money kept by corrupt Indians in Swiss banks. That money would be so much that he would use it to deposit 1.5 million rupees into the account of every single Indian citizen, he said.

In 2023 when India overtook China as the world's most populous nation, there were 1.43 billion Indians. So, Modi promised money into peoples' accounts at 1.5 million rupees each multiplied by 1.43 billion people. This multiplication is far beyond what my simple brain can take. When you find out the correct answer, please let me know.

That 'woh toh sirf jumla tha', lollipop we offered you suckers, was given by Amit Shah, Modi's most important minister and hatchet man and the people of India still voted them in a second time in 2019 with an even larger majority.

25

THE INTANGIBLE HINDU DIVINITY

I am a defender of Hinduism and a critic of Hindutva, which forgets the far-ahead-of-its-times philosophy of the religion. Hindutva people, who call themselves Sanatani, ignore the spiritual aspect and focuses instead on blind ritual and foisting a distinct saffron self-identity to create Islamophobia.

Devdutt Pattanaik, a mythologist and writer, describes the hate spewed by Hindutva in a funny way. He says in a post on Facebook:

"Sanatani is a newly emerging sect within Hinduism with some very peculiar features: Their God punishes 'evil' people, like Biblical God Jehovah. They chant Veda meticulously but cannot translate even a verse.

"Their Shiva is never shown with family. He is busy showing six-packs. Their Ram is never shown with Sita. He is just searching for her with his bow. Their Krishna never dances Ras-Leela. He is busy telling Arjuna to fight. Their Hanuman is always angry, never happy.

"Their Durga has weapons to fight. Never shown with Lakshmi, or Saraswati. Their Ganesha is losing his belly and is preparing to go to war. Their Gods are only warriors, never dancers, musicians, teachers … no romance, no delight, no suspiciousness. Strange.

But Hinduism is diverse and includes everyone."

Hindus do not have one single holy book like the Quran or the Bible. We have thousands of holy books and an equal number of idols to worship. The Hindu god is not white like Jesus, nor blue like Krishna.

The Hindu divine is intangible, that which cannot be touched by any of the five human senses - the visual with eyes, the audible with ears, the olfactory with the nose, the taste with the tongue or the touch with the skin.

Each of these sensory stimulants are provided to you in a Hindu temple - the deity of Rama for the eyes, the temple bells for the ears, the smell of *karpur* incense for the nose, the *tirth* and *prasad* for the tongue and the touch of the temple doorstep or the *pujari* putting a *tikka* on you.

Hinduism says: Use each of your senses to focus on the atman, but take away one sensory input at a time, you may choose to replace Rama with a cow depending on your choice, then take away the temple bell and listen to a river flowing, in fact do away with the temple entirely, then replace the smell of *karpur* with the sweet fragrance of soil after the first rains.

You may replace each of these sensory inputs multiple times until you train your mind to go blank like a white screen in a cinema hall before the movie starts. Imagine an infant born in a movie theatre with shows on 24-hours day and night, non-stop.

The images and sounds on the cinema screen are exactly like our minds, the inputs keep coming in, more so in today's digital world, and you can never ever fathom that there is a pristine white screen to comprehend, only if you could cut off your mind projector, for one minute.

Words decoded:

Karpur : Camphor incense

Tirth   : Holy water

Prasad : Any sweet that is offered to a Hindu God and is then distributed among devotees

Pujari : A Hindu priest

Tikka   : Vermilion applied to the forehead

26

THE HINDUTVA BRIGADE MISUNDERSTANDS ME

They think if I am anti Modi, I am pro Rahul Gandhi. What nonsense! Meaning you can only have a black or a white and no greys in between, no wonder they do not get what Hinduism is.

Ask me what happened to me on June 4th, 2024, the day the Lok Sabha elections were announced.

Nothing extraordinary. I woke up at my usual semi-lazy hour of about 8 a.m. Fiddled over whether to have bread and butter or *chapati* with banana for breakfast.

Educated myself with all the intelligent opinion coming via my phone on NDA versus India, Modi versus *Pappu*, why markets will collapse if Pappu comes first, sorry *Shehzada* now. Closer to noon, I pondered over a light vodka if lunch would be good with dal, rice and papad or a fish curry rice with *kokam kadi* on the side.

By this time, many of my peers had pushed themselves over a nervous cliff side - my school mates, my first cousins, my neighbours who I have good relations with, all very close to me; Putting alarmist messages like Hindu Dharma is in danger.

I don't depend upon Shehzada or India alliance to protect my Hindu dharma that has flourished for more than 2,000 years. To me the election results will make no difference because I know whoever wins the race, I will still have to look after my own finances, my health and my peace.

I worry about my close ones who put all their stakes in Modi and a *Hindu Rashtra*, going the way of blind *Dhritarashtra* who destroyed dharma for *putra-moha*.

Words decoded:

Chapati	:	Wheat-flour dough rolled flat and round and fried on a pan
Pappu	:	Idiot, a name that the BJP gave to Rahul Gandhi
Shehzada	:	A Muslim Mughal empire prince that our prime minister uses in an insulting way to refer to Rahul Gandhi after Pappu turned out to be far more sharper than Modi could ever imagine.
Kokam Kadi	:	A tangy and salty beverage made from coconut flesh extract and garcinia indica, a sour fruit. It is picked in summers, crushed to extract its juice which is then sun dried along with the skin and salt. It's good to use all year round then.

Hindu Rashtra: Hindu nation

Dhritarashtra : The blind king who was patriarch of the Kaurava branch of the family that fought against their cousins, the Pandava, in the Mahabharat war.

Putra : Son

Moha : Love

27

PLAYING GAMES WITH *BHAKT* AND THE BARBRA EFFECT

I now play games with the *Bhakt* brigade because they get really annoyed at anything anti-Modi, it destroys their day, and I'm sure their emotions and health too when they are already battling diabetes and blood pressure. What they don't know is that I play with them, just to watch the fun. Like waving a saffron rag in front of a raging Hindutva bull and they go crazy.

While I go back to my serene life. Yes, I am concerned about Modi's autocratic ways and always believed that the people of India will show him his right place. Which they did in the June 2024 parliamentary elections and will do so in the future too.

I am no fan of the Congress or the Gandhi family either. I am a fan to myself, what with all this global warming and heat. I need my own dainty-looking Japanese fan, to wave myself cool. No one else will, not Modi, not Rahul.

Please keep entertaining me in my retired life: Come charging like a bull at me every time I hang here a saffron and poke fun at it.

Many of my well wishers cautioned me about writing on Modi, the BJP and Hindutva and said even if I did, I should round off the sharp edges to tone down the criticism. Another said I should show these parts of my book to a lawyer, all very caring suggestions because the Modi government has in the past gone after critics.

I hope that does not happen to me and if it does, I am optimistic that the Barbra effect will reward me richly. That is the famous singer and actor Barbra Streisand after whom is named a phenomenon that anyone trying to cover up anything makes it even more evident.

Actually, it is called the Streisand effect, but I took linguistic liberty because Barbra alliterated nicely with Bhakt. The celebrity filed a lawsuit in 2003 against photographer Kenneth Adelman, the founder of the California Coastal Records Project, who took pictures from a helicopter of the state's coastline.

He posted them on the Internet to raise public awareness on how environmental degradation was causing coastal erosion. Among the more than 12,000 photos that Adelman said was a not-for-profit effort meant for government agencies to use for scientific research, there was one picture in which Streisand's mansion appeared. She sued the photographer for $50 million saying the picture violated her privacy.

At the time the lawsuit was filed, the photograph had been downloaded only six times, including twice by Streisand's lawyers. The case was highly publicised and was at once viewed more than 400,000 times. Streisand lost the suit, was ordered to pay Adelman legal fees, and the picture stays widely downloaded on the Internet.

Words decoded:

Bhakt : Devotee/follower. In political terms it refers to those who are blind Modi supporters

28

THE REAL PRACTICALITY
OF ANCIENT HINDU RITUAL

Now don't get me wrong. Every single Hindu ritual or practise had a practical point to it when first formulated. Reality is the reasons for which the rituals were prescribed no longer exist, but people still blindly follow them.

The *griha pravesh* with its pungent *homa* fire with *karpur* incense and other elements were our entry-point pest control then. It drove away all insects and flies in tropically hot Bharat. The annual *Satya Narayana puja* was the annual maintenance contract on pest control, while also making it a spiritually enriching experience at a time when people understood the Sanskrit shloka.

After my *munj* thread ceremony in 1975 at the age of 15, I was instructed to do the *sandhya* three times in a day: pratah kala-morning; madhyanah kala-noon and sayana kala evening.

I said I was instructed to do so, I never said I did it.

But I remember the ritual and the practicality behind it. You started with three aachman, sipping holy water from your palm to each of the first three incantations: 'Aum *Keshavaya* Namaha, Aum *Madhavaya* Namah, Aum *Narayana* Namaha'.

On the fourth chant, you took your palm full of water and sprinkled it around your banana leaf meal plate to create a slender wall of water so insects would not creep on into your food. Then you placed one morsel outside the boundary for them to eat and continued to eat yourself while reciting the balance 105 names out of the total 108.

How wonderful! Cannot think of a philosophy more inclusive - *Sarva dharma, Samabhav,* which can also be said as 'Sarva *prani,* sarva *keeda,* sambhav.

Vastu was the same; you placed the kitchen fire close to a window with the wind coming from the door or window opposite because the embers and smoke would go out. If you put it reverse, your lady love cooking for you, would either die of asthma or burns.

Today's vastu, if you do not want your neighbours to see your nude silhouette as you bathe at night in your bathroom under a yellow light, involves careful thought on the placement of the bulb.

Words decoded:

Griha pravesh   : A sacred ritual upon moving into a new home

Homa   : A sacrificial fire around which puja is done

Puja	: A sacred ritual to propitiate Gods, or one particular God
Karpur	: Camphor
Satya Narayana	: The true all-pervading God, Lord Vishnu
Munj	: Thread ceremony in which a Brahmin boy is initiated into learning the Veda, sacred books
Kala	: Time
Aum	: Not assets under management but an invocation to God
Namaha	: Divine presence
Keshavaya, Madhavaya, Narayana	: Three of 108 names of Lord Krishna, an avatar of Vishnu
Sarva	: All, all inclusive
Dharma	: Faith, religion
Samabhav	: Same, equivalent
Sarva Dharma Sambhav	: All religions are equal
Keeda	: Worm

29

JOURNALISM IS NOW "SNACK-ABLE CONTENT"

I don't mean to be a crabby old man saying: 'Oh, those were the good old days", you know! But some things have changed for sure like religion, mindless ritual, and journalism too.

In my simpler years as a motorcycle riding reporter, I only knew of news, opinion, and advertising and each was clearly segregated. Now there is an unholy mix of all three that they call 'content', which MBA-type media managers now further classify into brand-infused content, docu-stories, perishable news content repurposed to monetise later and the funniest of all - snack-able content.

I learnt it is byte-sized, or bite-sized, content that you consume quickie on your mobile phone - snippets on Bollywood, cricket, sex or TV anchors screaming Modi is restoring Ram Rajya.

Now most evenings over my whisky and soda, I look for tasty 'snack-able content'.

In this murky media world of today, international wire agencies such as Reuters and Bloomberg where I worked as an editor stand out for their integrity and it is economics that allow them the freedom to be an independent observer and commentator on the world around us.

At these agencies, unsourced stories are very rarely allowed and everything has to be attributed to a named source. On the few occasions that a story has to go out without attribution to protect the source, the reporter has to reveal the name to the team editor who if he or she thought passed muster, sent it up the chain for approval by a regional editor with a mandate for all for Asia. In my case that editor was Reinie Booysen, a most amiable South African. A top-class professional and better-still human being, he is now training editor for Bloomberg, Asia.

All these international news agencies invest hugely in training their journalists, which is how they get world-beating content that banks, major brokerages and financial institutions trust is totally independent and can be depended on to take bets worth millions of dollars on the equities, foreign exchange, bonds and commodities markets.

This live news feed along with realtime price feeds from markets around the world and historical data that they pack into their terminals along with analytics enable traders to compare yields of let us say Bundesbank German bonds versus Japanese Samurai bonds over a 10-year period in a matter of minutes.

All this put together make Reuters and Bloomberg feeds invaluable to financial professionals who take big time bets on the markets and subscription rates for a single Bloomberg terminal are at $30,000 (25,42,000 rupees) a year. For customers with two or more terminals, Bloomberg charges $26,580 per year.

A Reuters terminal, now renamed Refinitiv Eikon, costs $22,000 a year. A single Bloomberg terminal's cost each day translates to nearly 7,000 rupees. A Times of India newspaper in Mumbai is sold for eight rupees, which means what you pay for a Bloomberg for one day can buy you the Times of India for 28 months. And you get a bonus when you sell the newspaper to recyclers at the rate of 20 rupees a kilo.

Newspapers of the Times of India group, of Anand Bazaar Patrika group and TV channels depend upon advertising for survival and are in no position to be critical of anyone powerful, least of all the government of Prime Minister Modi.

On the other hand, international news agencies earn billions in subscriptions from around the globe and can afford to be truly independent. As is the case with Reuters and Bloomberg, places that I enjoyed working as a journalist.

Words decoded:

Ram Rajya : A nation state of perfect justice with good and righteous governance as existed during the rule of Lord Ram

30

A GERIATRIC TREE OFFICER

One of the pitfalls of saying you are retired is enthusiastic Mumbai co-operative housing society members quickly enlist you into the 'managing committee' to do all things from paying bills to getting garbage clearing done and managing municipality permission for 'tree-trimming'.

It is not as simple as hair-trimming because my head and hair belong to me, while trimming trees belongs to the Brihanmumbai Municipal Corporation, BMC. Under section 8, read along with Section 21 of the Maharashtra (urban areas) Tree Protection and Preservation Act, 1975, which comes under the overarching umbrella of the 'National Green Mission', there are extremely strict rules on which tree you can touch.

It may have grown wild in the rains; branches may fall in gusty winds, breaking a building beam or next-door Uncle Pereira's shoulder blade. Whatever! You must give an application on the letter head of Divine Society in Goregaon East, properly authorised with a round rubber stamp, BMC says.

They do not give permission and 'Junior Tree Officer' from BMC, says if I do this without permission, I will break rules under Section 8, read along with Section 21 of Facebook's rules on tree privacy.

I say: "I will do that for sure. But do not send me to a 'Junior Tree Officer', because the trees I wish to cut are all very senior and either dying or dead." I need to talk to a 'Senior Tree Officer", or better still, a 'Geriatric Tree Officer'.

'Okay," they say to me in Marathi, *Tumhee patra liha* '.

Words decoded:

Tumhee   :   You

Patra   :   Letter

Liha   :   Write

31

A GO-AIR FLIGHT THAT WENT NOWHERE FOR THREE HOURS

When I am not writing letters to municipal authorities, I try and travel whenever there is spare cash, which is not very often. One April Fool's Day, I was stuck at Dabolim Airport in Goa because my flight to Mumbai was delayed by a full three hours.

The reason given by the Goan girls at the Go Air counter was the most bizarre I had ever heard. Just an update that Go Air now goes nowhere because they shut down in 2023. The incoming flight from Mumbai arrived on schedule but did not get permission to land and circled some six times in the lazy afternoon Goan air when the pilot saw he was low on fuel, they said.

He had a choice of continuing circling, hoping he would get to land just before his last drop of Aviation Turbine Fuel was sucked into his engines. But what if the Goan control tower staff did not come back in time from their afternoon *copa* and fish curry-rice. So, the pilot decided to return to Mumbai.

Now there were a whole bunch of howling passengers on that plane because they were shown a glimpse of Goa from the air and were being taken right back to Mumbai. There was another set of irate passengers on the ground in Goa, fed up with too much susegad, keenly desirous of going back to Mumbai.

A 65-plus man led the charge against the hapless Go Air staff at Dabolim Airport with the sharpness of someone who once held a big job. The man displayed sterling leadership qualities in gathering some 50-odd passengers in saying powerfully and most eloquently how the airline was hopeless.

Since his retirement he probably never had this kind of attention and once satisfied that his power was still intact, he retreated. Soon the others melted away too - some to sleep in a sulk on a plastic chair at the airport, some to stuff themselves with *laccha paratha* and some like me repairing to the bar to get a teeny-weeny bit of whisky and a healthy portion of butter chicken with jeera rice.

In a more meditative mood after that, I reckoned there must have been a 'Red Alert' of a potential security threat, which Intelligence and Security officials will not reveal to the public or the airline. Dabolim is a Defense airport controlled by the Indian Navy.

I felt sorry for the Go Air girls. So, after hearing their story one more time about the plane circling many times and running low on fuel, I said to them: *"Badal do, tumhara plane badal do"*. "Why Sir?" they asked and I said: *"Bahut kam de rahi hai! Mileage kam de rahi hai"*.

For the first time since their shift started that morning, they had a hearty laugh.

Words decoded:

Copa	:	Cup in Portuguese
Laccha Paratha	:	A multi-layered flat bread that is popular in North Indian cuisine
Badal do	:	You please change
Tumhara	:	Your, Yours
Bahut kam de rahi hai	:	Yielding very low mileage. Among intensely cost-conscious Indians, how much petrol a vehicle drinks is an important factor in determining which car or bike to buy. India's largest selling motorcycle maker, until recently when it was overtaken by Honda Motors, had an advertising line that said: "Fill it, Shut it, Forget it."

32

MAIYA TO MASALA TO MONEY

MTR is the now shortened acronym of Mavalli Tiffin Room set up by the Maiya family in Bangalore in 1924. Its turning point from a single stand-alone restaurant to a food giant came when patriarch Yagnanarayana Maiya took an ethical stand that he would not lower his quality under any circumstances.

That was in 1975 when Indira Gandhi declared emergency and among other draconian steps conjured up a cap on how much restaurants could charge. The utterly low prices prescribed meant it was just not possible to provide food of the same quality - Maiya decided not to lower standards one bit, and he took losses each day that MTR served meals.

He did one unique thing - each day he put a board outside his restaurant at Lalbagh in Bangalore detailing the loss MTR has suffered that day and the cumulative losses below. Until one day the money lost was more than he could manage, and he put out a final board saying MTR was closing.

It closed the next day, but Maiya could not bear the thought of his employees losing their jobs. So, he retained all of them at work and asked them to focus on making dry masala powders to sell in packets in shops.

That is what eventually became MTR Foods, in which a Singapore-based private equity investor bought a 20% stake in Year 2000. Two years later, JP Morgan bought another 28% stake for $4 million. In 2007, Norwegian Orkla Ventures bought out MTR Foods entirely for $100 million.

So, you see, as long as you stay ethical and true to your beliefs like Maiya, good luck and fortune can strike you any moment, as long as you are open to it. I am hoping one of these days Lily from Bblunt makes it big, spots me across the road and says:

"Uncle, you made my career. I am starting a new salon chain called B-Old and you will be my brand ambassador."